the art of discernment

THE IGNATIAN IMPULSE SERIES

the art of discernment

making good decisions in your world of choices

Stefan Kiechle

ave maria press AMP Notre Dame, Indiana

www.avemariapress.com

International Standard Book Number: 1-59471-035-X

First published as *Sich entscheiden* in Germany in 2004 by Echter Verlag.

Cover and text design by Brian C. Conley

Printed and bound in the United States of America.

Library of Congress Cataloging-in-Publication Data
Kiechle, Stefan, 1960-
   [Sich Entscheiden. English]
   The art of discernment : making good decisions in your world of choices / Stefan Kiechle.
      p. cm. - - (The Ignatian impulse series)
   ISBN 1-59471-035-X (pbk.)
   1. Discernment (Christian theology) 2. Decision making- -Religious aspects- -Catholic Church. 3. Ignatius, of Loyola, Saint, 1491-1556. Exercitia spiritualia. I. Title. II. Series.

   BV4509.5.K46513 2005
   248.4- -dc22

                                    2004024242

Contents

CHAPTER ONE

"I'VE GOT A PROBLEM"

I have to make a decision now! My future depends on it. I'm about ready to give up hope because I just can't make up my mind. I'm torn apart by all the possibilities—and I'm still discovering more. Everything is so complicated, so confusing. Once I make a decision, there will be no turning back. One possibility appeals to me, but then another one won't let me go. I would love to keep my options open. I want to be completely certain before making any decision. I simply need more time. I wish I could simply put this decision off, but I'm under such pressure. Soon, I'll have to let people know what I really want to do.

My female and male friends offer me entirely different advice, making their opinions completely useless. In a way, all the alternatives frighten me. I have tried meditation and prayer, and they have helped me calm down a bit. But I really did not gain any new insight this way. And my mind is not helping me either, because I keep finding arguments for and against everything. And the time is flying by. If I don't say yes now, everything will slip away from me. But I simply cannot make up my mind yet. I'm afraid of the decision.

The purpose of this book is to help you make good personal decisions. Decisions are a necessary part of life. And there are so many throughout our lives: choosing a major, selecting a career, accepting a job, deciding whether or not to marry someone, picking a place to live, having children, pursuing certain leisure activities, resolving marital problems, becoming socially, politically, or religiously engaged. Even deciding when to decide can be a big decision. The ordinary everyday decisions regarding the many small things in life can also affect, form, and shape us.

Lots of people have a difficult time making decisions. What is a "right" decision? Where and how can one find criteria for it? Are there any methods, or even something like techniques, that can be helpful during the process of reflection and discernment? What kind of mistakes is one likely to make and how can one avoid making them? When is a decision clear-cut?

These and similar questions are the subject of this book. It is particularly directed at people who seek to incorporate spirituality into their decisions. Those who take a spiritual approach to decision making may well ask themselves if and how this reliance on spirituality will lead them to good and right decisions. We will explore the spiritual tradition of discernment developed by Ignatius of Loyola, who has always been considered a specialist in such matters. One chapter will specifically focus on him. After that, we will introduce criteria and methods of discernment based on his teaching. A special chapter will deal with most common difficulties. Finally, the book will conclude with guidelines that summarize Ignatius' approach and which will help readers apply it to real life situations. But first, let us take a look at the problems inherent to discernment.

A WORLD OF DECISIONS

The world we live in has become very complicated. The possibilities it offers are nearly unlimited, each with its own particular advantages and disadvantages. This fascinates us and irritates us, excites us and frightens us. Because the possibilities and consequences are intertwined, every decision creates repercussions that are not directly connected to it. For instance, if one accepts a new job, one may have to move to another city with all the consequences such a move will have for you and your family and friends. Once a couple decides to have a baby, they may have to redefine their job situation or their future careers. What might be an advantage in one area frequently leads to a disadvantage in another area.

The long-term consequences of a decision are often impossible to anticipate. They are full of risk, they make us insecure, anxious, even fearful. In most cases, we can determine only much later if the decision was right, and this subsequent weighing of the pros and cons can renew our doubts. And what about wrong decisions? They make us lose valuable time, reduce the quality of our lives, or may even damage us for the rest of our lives. We can hardly afford to make mistakes in our performance-oriented culture. How can we make decisions in an atmosphere of greater trust, calm, and certainty?

Our multifaceted world is like a marketplace offering thousands of possibilities. The advertising industry persuades us, in ways that we are not even aware of, to make decisions. It promises us infinite happiness, albeit in a dream world of virtual reality. In the end, we want *everything*—which is, of course, clearly impossible. Therefore, we must make decisions, and we must make them in the real world. It is at this point that many people founder. The difficulties inherent in making decisions are overwhelming. They end up refusing to come to a decision and thus miss out on their lives. Or they reach decisions they will have to reverse later on. The results are separations and broken relationships. Of course, these are all a part of human existence. Yet failures resulting from faulty decisions are particularly painful and often no longer curable because of the guilt associated with them.

For their own purposes, advertisers take advantage of that universal longing that is part of human nature, a longing that extends beyond all temporal affairs. It is a spiritual longing. What we want is fullness, paradise, heaven. Thus we hope that we will obtain in heaven everything we long for with a pure heart. However, in the here and now, we are limited and we must be content with getting only a fraction of what we desire. That is hard on us because it contradicts the natural tendencies of our hearts. Like Adam and Eve, we really want to be like God. But the fact is that we are human, limited both physically and spiritually, and moving ever closer to the end of our lives. Is that merely a burden, or is it possible to discover in it both happiness and fulfillment?

Anybody making a decision affirms one thing while denying another. Many people forget to consciously include the no. Unless the no is equally executed with the yes, the result will be dissatisfying. When this occurs we tend to keep lamenting the possibility we did not select, as if it were something that we once had, but lost. In order to avoid that hurt and distress, many people simply put off making decisions. They want to keep all their options open, and so they wait until—without their noticing it—it is too late. All that's left is to bemoan the missed opportunity.

Friends and acquaintances will usually applaud us when we make a decision, but sometimes even they will not be supportive if they don't understand our reasons. By coming to a particular decision, we create a certain image of ourselves, an identity of sorts. From now on, a certain woman will be identified with being a teacher, a banker, or a nun. Someone gets married and is now identified with his or her spouse's idiosyncrasies—both strengths and weaknesses. Such is the image we present of ourselves to the public. What will others think of us? Are we happy with the image our acquaintances are forming of us in their minds? There will be the occasional friend who will turn away from us, and that may hurt. But—hopefully—we will also make new friends. Thus, even with regard to our social identity, we assume untold risks when we make decisions.

WHEN BOTH MIND AND HEART ARE AT ODDS

I'm tempted to do something completely crazy. I want to leave my predictable lifestyle and all its rituals behind. The restrictions of my job are getting to me. Maybe I should take off and spend a year in India. Or even stay there for the rest of my life. My emotions pull me in one direction, but then I realize that this is totally irrational. People say that I am going to mess up my future.

Of course, my own sentiments are contradictory too, a mixture of desire and fear. Am I being drawn by a pleasant, but temporary, dream? How can I determine what is really going on? Do normal and rational mean only those things that an average middle-class person strives for, those things one can be sure of? Is a career always preferable? Honestly, my heart can't distinguish clearly, and what is worse, I'm unable to get my rational self to cooperate with my heart. How am I going to find a way out of this jungle?

Some people approach things rationally. Everything has to be thoroughly reasoned out and organized. Their mind provides a reasonable explanation for every single thing they do. But does the mind always get to the core of the matter? Aren't the explanations sometimes highly contrived? And aren't feelings frequently brushed aside? Perhaps they are not sensitive enough to recognize them. Things can get pretty unpleasant if one is seemingly guided by strong emotions without being able to admit this fact to others or to oneself. Beneath what appear to be clever rationalizations, there may sometimes be hidden a driven human being. Rational people frequently use willpower to achieve their goals. They define objectives rationally and subsequently pursue them with great efficiency. Our modern world appreciates that sort of behavior. Still, people who rely on purely rational decisions frequently dismiss from their calculations aspects of reality that contradict their own theoretical thinking. Standing firm, they do not waver in the face of facts or the advice of others. How can people who approach everything rationally avoid these traps? Is there any way to use this gift to analyze complicated situations and circumstances rationally while still connecting to our emotions?

Other people are ruled by their emotions; they approach everything from an emotional angle. Their behavior is dictated by strong emotions, oftentimes in a way that they are not even aware of. External events arouse strong feelings in them, provoking rather unpredictable reactions. Emotional people often demonstrate a warm heart, are easily approachable, and are therefore thought to be congenial. But sometimes they are subject to mood swings. When it comes to making decisions, their feelings may point in the right direction, but they can also deceive, proposing unreal fears or starry-eyed dreams. Psychological stress and hurtful past experiences can also shape their emotional life in ways that distort their perception of the real world. Emotional people are capable of blocking out reality and hiding behind their strong emotions. They are even capable of immunizing themselves almost completely from obvious facts and the advice of others. How can emotional people avoid such traps? How can they keep themselves from simply drifting along complacently? Is there a way for them to use this valuable gift of their emotions in the process of decision making in a partnership with reason?

Another way of looking at how our psychology affects our decision making is to distinguish between people who are ruled by the heart and those who are ruled by the gut. People who follow their heart display strong feelings and moods toward others and are more likely influenced by external events. Their hearts waver frequently, they experience doubts and tend to hesitate, or they are inspired and propelled by their hearts. People who follow their gut have a strong physical presence. They react intuitively, are frequently rather single-minded and action oriented, as if they were driven more by their instinct.

This typology of personalities and differentiation of them according to different psychological models could be developed further, but for now, it may suffice to acknowledge that our personality type affects the way we approach the decision-making process. Each of us must learn how to deal with the weaknesses and strengths of our particular character. We must learn to recognize the traps we face and avoid them. We carry within us the desire to integrate ever more completely our rational self and our emotional life, our heart and our gut, our senses and our mind. The further we advance down this long path of human maturation, the easier it will be to make decisions. And yet, as we move along, we are forced to continuously make decisions in the midst of our very real imperfections and fragility.

THE ISSUE OF TIME

One person may say: *I felt constant pressure to make up my mind about a job offer. I'm torn, and in spite of racking my brains, I'm stuck. I've been hesitating for days, unable to make up my mind. It seems like every time I'm supposed to come up with a decision, I have this same problem. Maybe I chose the wrong major back in college, but I can't just start all over again. It's too late for that now. The past is the past. But what is to become of me?*

Another person may say: *I decided immediately to take the job. I never make a big deal about things like that. I know right away what I want and then I just move full speed ahead. But later, I started having doubts. Was I perhaps too rash? If I quit now people will think that I'm a failure. How will that look on my resume? And what will my friends think of me? Those who tried to dissuade me from taking this job will think they were right. They'll gloat and I'll have to hide from them. What will become of me then?*

The first person lacks resolve. He or she puts off decisions, probably for fear of making the wrong decision. People like that always believe that they have not gotten to the bottom of every single complication and thus cannot yet make up their mind. They are afraid of taking risks; they want to be absolutely certain. Yet, with every new insight they uncover new questions. There are a lot of people who cannot make up their minds and thus put off decisions affecting their life. They may postpone getting married or settling down in a job. Some of these postponements are caused by complex social relationships and economic realities, but others are simply neglected or postponed until it is too late.

The second type of person is determined to force the issue. He or she insists on clearing up matters instantly without allowing for sufficient time to weigh the pros and cons. These people either do not know or do not appreciate the fact that the soul requires a certain time to mature before there can be clarity about what it needs or wants. Rushing a decision may impress others with how self-assured and strong one is, yet hidden beneath this decisiveness there is often a deep-seated fear of weakness of the complicated world that lacks clarity. Unresolved situations are considered intolerable and the risks involved in reaching a decision are thought to be less if one rushes it. If, however, the decision turns out later to be wrong, one feels even more insecure and ridiculous, a failure.

What do we need to do in order to determine the appropriate time for reaching a decision? According to the way in which the ancient Greeks perceived time, there is a distinction between *kairos*, when we intuitively sense the proper moment, and *chronos*, i.e., objective, linear time. Nowadays, *chronos* appears to be controlling us, pushing us ever faster and ever more relentlessly. Captured by *chronos*, we are prevented from achieving *kairos*. The progression of time vexes us so much that we feel pressured, no longer free. How will we be able to find the proper time frame for making decisions? How are we going to harmonize the pressing external demands with the internal, decidedly slower rhythm?

At times, we experience just the opposite: Deep inside, we sense the urge to clear up matters as soon as possible, yet the external circumstances remain unclear and confused. The cause is frequently our encounter with widely scattered fears that both disturb our sense of time and force us into either making premature decisions or delaying them. The fear to do something wrong or at the wrong time compounds the situation and fuels new fears.

WHAT ABOUT THE WILL OF GOD?

Prior to making decisions, believers ask themselves about what God wants them to do. In earlier times, people asked this question because they were afraid of being punished by God if they did not do his will. Thankfully, our view of God has changed: We ask about God's will because we believe that he has only our best interests in mind. Therefore, if we recognize God's will and act accordingly, we will choose the best of all possibilities. That is why we must strive to determine God's will. Yet how are we to go about that?

I'm beginning to wonder if God wants something different from me than what I want for myself. I'm a surgeon and would like to accept a new position at a prestigious hospital. However, I have also been invited to assist with an aid project in Africa for a couple years under rather primitive conditions. I don't feel at all like accepting this. However, is it possible that God is asking me to do this work? Must I follow his will? Why would he want me to choose this path? And if he is, what will happen if I don't obey?

Devout Christians impress us because they are deeply guided by their faith, even to the point of leading a different life. They orient their lives to God and make their decisions based on faith. Many people are searching for ways of combining their faith with decisions about their lives. Yet they find that it is not so simple for them as it may appear to be for others. Questions such as these arise, and they can be difficult to answer:

- Is God's will directed at the individual human being in the sense that he demands from every individual one thing, and one thing only?
- How can one recognize the desire of God that one can hope will lead to good?
- What will it take to translate this will into action purposefully and vigorously?
- Can we base our decision making on prayer for counsel and assistance?
- How can the Bible help us in this endeavor?
- Is there anything else that may help us to successfully combine faith with those ever-necessary decisions about life?
- How will we find our way, relying as it were on our Christian ideals and principles, in a highly specialized world that seems to be so infinitely remote from God?

Questions such as these are multifaceted and probe deep into our lives. In this little book we will only be able to touch upon the issues involved in resolving such questions. Yet, if this book helps just a few readers with the difficult challenge of making decisions, it will fulfill its purpose.

CHAPTER TWO

IGNATIUS OF LOYOLA, OUR GUIDE

Ignatius of Loyola lived during the first half of the sixteenth century. He descended from an old Basque noble family that was dedicated to the knightly ideals of the late Middle Ages. After receiving a serious war injury, Ignatius changed his life. A long spiritual search with many detours eventually brought him to the realization that he was called to become a priest and "help souls." He studied in Paris as well as in various cities of Spain. Together with a small group of companions, he founded a religious order in Rome. This order developed a new pastoral style, calling itself the Society of Jesus, popularly referred to as the Jesuits. Until his death, Ignatius guided the community that rejected monastic elements and dedicated all its efforts to ministry, mission, and education. The Jesuits refrained from becoming tied to specific places. They remained mobile and at the direction of the Pope were sent all over the world. By the time of Ignatius' death, the order was growing rapidly and already had a thousand members. Through the vicissitudes of history, the order has continued to live the vision of Ignatius. Today, there are approximately twenty thousand members working on every continent.

IGNATIUS AND THE MODERN WORLD

In Ignatius' time, Europe was in turmoil. Historians refer to this period as the beginning of the modern age. During the Middle Ages technology and the economy had advanced to the point where people had become more mobile. They traveled more and came into contact with different cultures. The discovery of the New World opened up unknown and vast horizons. Christian Europe did not make up the entire world. Now there was a broad awareness that different civilizations, despite the fact that they were pagan, were in some ways culturally superior. This shattered the self-image of the "Old World" and roused its curiosity. The reality of the known world had become fluid: the constants, both large and small, were changing as new things were discovered. Individuals had to constantly adapt themselves, increase their knowledge, and reorient their horizon. And they had to make decisions.

The rise of the Modern Age was accompanied by the emergence of the individual. An increasingly urbanized world demanded individuals with strong personalities who would pursue various professions and lifestyles that could be chosen depending on social status and talent. The social groups became more transparent. To a certain degree, hard work and luck could raise a person's status in society, whereas bad luck and a lack of talent could prompt a move in the opposite direction. Individuals were personally challenged to work and to become creatively engaged, requiring them to make ever new decisions. During the Middle Ages, pretty much everything was predetermined by one's family and social background: one's educational opportunities, one's profession, one's spouse, and one's position within the church. This continuous process of social and cultural change gradually ushered in what came to be known as the modern world. Ignatius was caught in the midst of these changes.

Throughout the Middle Ages people's lives were characterized by a predetermined orderliness. Now life became more chaotic. Much had to be newly classified, ordered, developed, shaped and, therefore, decisions had to be made. All of a sudden, the individual—at first, mostly men—were responsible for decisions. Ethics, the teachings about proper conduct, became the dominating theme in the modern age. Soon, the question about the will of God was raised: Are we merely drifting through life without direction? Are there any goals or objectives? Does God predetermine them? Does he possess a will of his own? Clearly, there was and still exists a problem with how one can determine in the midst of life's chaos what God wants. This dilemma applies equally to individuals who ask, "What is my calling?" and to communities who ask, "What should we do?" For instance, Ignatius asked this question on behalf of a young man who was facing a decision affecting his entire life: Should I live in complete poverty, perhaps even enter a religious order? And he asked the same question on behalf of his entire order: Which pastoral tasks should we take on and which should we decline to take on? Where will we find work that will be more important and more fruitful?

In his *Spiritual Exercises*, Ignatius developed a spiritual pedagogy whose purpose was, among other things, to assist people in making decisions that would affect them for the rest of their lives. In the following, several guidelines designed in the *Spiritual Exercises* will be highlighted. Because both the language and the imagery of the *Spiritual Exercises* are antiquated and difficult to understand, we will attempt to make them understandable for people living in the twenty-first century.

ON MAKING ONESELF "INDIFFERENT"

I have always wanted to enter politics. Just thinking about it is exciting. I could do a lot of good; I could shape society in accordance with my own ideals and, in doing so, make a name for myself. Of course, I keep experiencing fear and I feel unsure of myself. Maybe I should become a teacher. I am equally attracted to this profession and, besides, it would be a sure thing. Yet isn't teaching rather frustrating? Besides, it wouldn't really help me if I'm trying to make it big. What am I really looking for, deep down?

Every human being clings to certain things while instinctively rejecting others. At times, a certain task that seems interesting and desirable entices us, while a different one turns us off; we don't like it, it makes us apprehensive, and we come up with a thousand reasons for not doing it, sidestepping it instead. Similarly, we frequently find certain people attractive and congenial—or not, and thus avoid them. Ignatius talks about the "motions" of the soul: affection and preferences as well as aversions, fears, and defensive reactions. These motions are affective, marked by strong feelings. Still, thoughts and arguments play an important role, too; frequently, both elements intimately affect one another.

Ignatius teaches us to become "indifferent" when we come face to face with a decision. This strategy encourages us to pay attention to and examine the motions of the heart. If we do that, we will recognize that in some of the motions of our hearts, we are seeking our own personal advantage, while in others we remain selfless, seeking the advantage of others, or even everybody's. Someone who would be entirely indifferent would have completely freed himself or herself of self-serving motions. Since we will never succeed in doing so, "indifferent" means above all that we will not permit the latter motions to influence our decisions—Ignatius refers to these as "disordered" because they bring disharmony and chaos into our lives (Saint Ignatius of Loyola, *Spiritual Exercises* as taken from the *Spiritual Exercises of St. Ignatius,* translation and commentary by George E. Ganss, S.J.; Chicago: Loyola University Press, 1992. Paragraph number 21. All following references will be abbreviated SE with the paragraph number following, which is consistent in any edition of the *Spiritual Exercises*).

Of course, this is easier said than done. If we allowed ourselves no longer to be determined at all by forms of self-centeredness, we would be saintlier than the saints. It is already difficult enough to recognize and assess well the motions in our hearts. Mindful of this problem, Ignatius developed lessons that he referred to as the "discernment of spirits." Thus we must practice discernment throughout our lives, and grow in the necessary experience. Therefore, those people who recognize their "disordered" state, who keep ridding themselves of it, will approach their decisions with greater indifference, even if it will be impossible to completely implement this strategy.

A certain degree of this inner freedom—which is how indifference is translated most accurately—is an absolute condition for making good decisions. Only those who are free, according to this definition, can avoid becoming trapped by the urge to seek only their own benefit, and thus end up imprisoned by their very egos. Only those who practice inner freedom will be able to ask which among all the countless possibilities will realize the greater good. Only those who are free will possess enough distance from themselves to make it possible for them to make a decision based on substantive criteria and values instead of simply following their spontaneous feelings or thoughts.

Ignatius describes indifference as a state where people no longer desire health more than sickness, wealth more than poverty, a long life more than a short life, honor more than dishonor, but instead they desire what brings them closer to the "end for which [they] are created" (SE 23). Therefore, one ought to be prepared to accept personal setbacks if they benefit a higher goal. As simple as this advice may seem, it is nevertheless an unheard of challenge. Being Christians, we stand up for other people and are prepared to set aside our personal advantages and accept suffering. Ultimately, indifference means to *be free of* disordered attachments to personal goods and the freedom to *devote our lives to* a greater general good.

ON BEING FREE OF . . .

I think I'll become a banker. I could make good money and it would be a great career. I'll look good in the eyes of others and I will be in charge of a lot things. Somehow, the thought of cleverly taking advantage of other people's weaknesses excites me. And I'll be able to buy a lot of things for myself with all the money I make. My empty feeling, this nagging feeling of inadequacy, will finally go away and I'll be able to stand tall and powerful.

I'm attracted to this woman. I've got to have her. I don't know why but she turns me on. It would be a blast to be seen in her company. My friends would

look up to me; that would show them. They'll for-
get all about my earlier insults. Plus, she's rich! I
won't have to worry about money anymore.

Most of us probably don't consciously think like these people. And yet, all of us harbor within us these same thought patterns, whether consciously or unconsciously, or more or less explicitly. People who yield to these desires place themselves and their needs above all other things. They say "I" in every sentence they utter. They are not interested in other people, but use them for their own purposes. They are determined to climb the social or corporate ladder at the expense of others, and may even be driven by some hidden resentment. Or they may repress their feelings of inferiority or fear and dominate other people in order to reach the top themselves. It is also possible that people like this will take out their own past hurts on others and do harm to them. Perhaps their most important values are money, power, sex, security, or their personal sense of honor and esteem.

In the *Spiritual Exercises*, Ignatius calls the first phase of the discernment process the First Week. Its purpose is to overcome "disordered affections." These can be directly and clearly self-centered inclinations, but these can also be subtle mechanisms of the soul that will be uncovered

only after a thorough and radically honest examination. Here, one must distinguish clearly
between good and evil. This decision is not truly
free because we are morally obligated to decide
in favor of good.

In addition to self-centeredness proper—
referred to as "sin" in theological terms—fears
and injuries also play a role on this journey
toward liberation. Whenever we encounter genuine danger or harm, fears serve as helpful
warning signals to the soul. Still, fears can be
irrational and out of proportion. When this hap-
pens they will confine and enslave us; we must
then try to see through them and overcome them
by establishing trusting relationships with others
and with God. People truly possessed by fear
sometimes need to pursue a course of therapy.

Injuries that have not healed can be deeply
rooted in the soul and interfere with making free
decisions. They can lead to exaggerated fears of
new injuries or to inordinately aggressive or
hostile behavior. Sometimes they lead—unconsciously—to lashing out at innocent people.
Frequently, if a person appears to be bad tem-
pered, the cause is a hurt he or she had suffered
without ever having had an opportunity to
process it, and so now he or she simply passes it
on. Many injuries can be healed through trust,
conversation, and prayer. Of course, severe psychological injury calls for therapy.

But back to the subject of sin: Prior to making any decisions, we ought to make an effort to see through the disordered inclinatons in our soul. We will be frightened by them and may feel ashamed. Each attempt at eradicating them with psychological tricks or by force will fail. On the contrary, we ought to accept them. But accepting them does not mean that we ought to yield to them. Rather, it means that we understand them respectfully and with a sense of humor, recognizing that they are part of us and then ridding ourselves of them. They must influence our actions as little as possible. Since we recognize also pure and "ordered" inclinations during self-examination, we can pattern our decisions accordingly.

Is it possible simply to remove disordered inclinations from the soul? The practices of classical spirituality possess an entire arsenal of ascetic exercises making that attempt. Nowadays, as a result of psychological insights, we take a skeptical view of such attempts at self-discipline. And yet, people know instinctively the ways in which they can promote or fight their disordered desires. That is why Ignatius warns repeatedly to knowingly "steer counter" to the temptations. We ought to particularly trust and pray that *God* will remove in due course from our hearts what is disordered and simultaneously bring about genuine conversion. We don't become saints by our own doing but by God's grace.

People who are cultivating a spiritual awareness experience themselves as accepted by God. God's acceptance includes the forgiveness of every evil in us. Though God does not accept our sins, he will accept us, even though we are sinners. The experience of God's forgiveness feels like balm for the soul. It helps the sinner better to accept himself; it heals the soul from the bottom up.

ON BEING FREE TO . . .

I'm torn. I can either study languages and eventually work in an international agency doing development work, or I could pursue biology and use that knowledge to help shape the future in ways that will benefit humanity. I've thoroughly examined myself and I can't find anything bad or evil in either option. Both would be good alternatives, both fit with my Christian faith. But how am I going to figure out which course of study I ought to select?

I've always thought about entering a monastery. But now I've fallen in love. All my plans have gotten mixed up. I was passionately attracted to the religious life and now something entirely different has been kindled inside of me. I'm incredibly attracted to both. Why can't I combine them? Both alternatives are good choices in the eyes of God. How am I to determine God's specific wishes? What does he want me to do?

These people are each in a dilemma, facing two genuine and good alternatives. If there were any disordered inclinations in their hearts, they have been gotten rid of a long time ago. Both alternatives could be the right path to follow and lead to personal peace. Both could be God's will—there is obviously no reason to reject either one them. The point here is to discern between good and better.

Ignatius refers to choice only in this context. The choice is truly *free* because one can decide either way. If we choose to select the better alternative—whose criteria are yet to be considered—we will be in an ever *better* position to realize our destiny.

In his *Spiritual Exercises*, Ignatius calls this phase of the discernment process the Second Week. During this week, we practice how to ponder and weigh the choices well. What will be important is our ability to recognize the alternatives and the motions in favor of and against each alternative. This may appear self-evident, yet it won't be easy in practical terms to drop all prejudices, accept all pieces of information as value-free, face reality free of fear and openly, and honestly view all feelings and thoughts with a calm or enthusiastic heart. It requires us to acknowledge the truth inherent to both inner and external realities.

After having faced and accepted the truth, we must judge. As Christians, we are surrounded by a spiritual tradition that is supposed to assist us and point us in the right direction. Yet learning how to apply it to our lives in every new instance is a challenge. According to Ignatius, decisions cannot only or always be deduced from general moral principles. We must heed our unique inner voice. Subjectivity yields information about what is better. By listening to our hearts we hear the hidden will of God. The next chapter will provide several criteria for the proper ways of doing this.

In his *Spiritual Exercises,* Ignatius introduces us to the primary—and perhaps the most important—strategy that will show us how to be free: looking at Jesus. His life is our example and our standard: his mercy and his faithfulness, his truthfulness and his courage, his magnanimity and his love. Again and again, Ignatius recommends to us to meditate on and study the life and works of Jesus. By establishing and deepening an inner relationship with Jesus, his person and his deeds, we are "shaped" by him, and our lives subsequently gain clarity and depth.

THE THREE WAYS OF MAKING CHOICES

Ignatius offers a few limited, but important, hints regarding the problem of whether to pay more attention to the mind or the heart, whether to favor extended, careful deliberation or simply listen to intuition (SE 175–177). He distinguishes three ways of making choices, which are executed at different occasions.

First, Ignatius describes direct intuition as the primary form of discernment. In a kind of sudden calling, one experiences a direct, divine inspiration that clarifies unquestionably what needs to be done. A typical example is Saul's calling on the road to Damascus. Divine lightning knocked him to the ground; the experience completely changed him and converted him into Paul, the fervent missionary to a Christianity that was still in its infancy (Acts 9:1–20). Most people consider events such as this highly rare and even slightly peculiar. Can they be trusted? Is there any way to find out if they are genuine? Perhaps events of this type are more frequent than one would commonly assume. Ignatius presupposes a person who is on a search, has a relationship with God, and is therefore open to this type of experience. Of course, there is no way that one would ever be able to bring it about by oneself since it is a gift: sudden, unexpected, and undeserved.

The second method of making choices is to notice inclinations and to distinguish among them. Inclinations are primarily affections. One observes them and deduces from them the proper path. The Ignatian "discernment of the spirits" is based on this method of selection. What is most important above all are the feelings that surface during the course of honest and calm meditation and prayerful enumeration of the alternatives. It is here that the Spirit is able to act, but so is the anti-spirit who needs to be distinguished from the Spirit.

The third method of discernment is selected whenever the inclinations do not quite seem to get going, that is, whenever feelings reveal nothing or very little. This is the rational approach to making decisions: The arguments in favor of or against each alternative are examined and the reasons are carefully weighed. Then the sum total and the importance of the various arguments will point toward the solution.

Ignatius, whom many people have falsely accused of being rationalistic and "brainy," considered the third, rational method of discernment as a course of last resort to achieve the desired purpose. Experience, however, illustrates that decisions are frequently the result of a combination between the second and third approach to making decisions. We examine expressions of emotion *and* arguments; we listen to our inner inclinations and disinclinations regarding the possibilities *and* we examine the alternatives objectively as to their respective advantages and disadvantages. Both methods ought to complement, merge, and affirm one another. Finally, we can hope—although this is impossible to achieve outright—that the sense of intuition described in the first method of discernment will confirm our decision. We can hope for an intuitive flash of truth beyond all doubt; a bright, divine inspiration that will motivate us, make us enthusiastic, and advance the level of discernment.

Should we select one of the three methods of discernment whenever we are facing decisions? The answer is both yes and no. No, because the favorable conditions of a given moment of time will send us in the direction of one of the methods of discernment. At times our feelings offer clear advice, at other times it will be our mind, and sometimes it will be a flash from heaven. This is to be our presumption. Depending on one's personality there may be a tendency to lean toward one method or another. But the answer is also yes because, up to a certain point, one can make an effort to try out the methods that do not seem to fit naturally. In the presence of strong feelings, one can also try to rely on the powers of the mind. Whenever the mind is extremely busy and points clearly in a certain direction, one can quietly but consciously examine feelings. As soon as a sudden intuition manifests itself, one should try to complement the intuition with feelings and arguments. If no intuition surfaces, one ought to also ask prayerfully for the gift of an intuitive signal. It is always a matter of an *also* here, because it goes without saying that every method of discernment can suffice on its own.

DISCERNMENT OF THE SPIRITS

I'm completely unsure about what to do. I'm actually a rather timid woman. Yet if I keep staring at my fears, I'll never be able to make a decision. Which fears should I pay attention to? Which should I ignore? Whenever I favor Alternative A, I anticipate my decision with particular joy. But how can I determine if this is a genuine kind of joy or merely a form of cheap comfort? Alternative B would be less predictable, but more exciting—or is it only my fondness of adventure? Alternative C would be the more difficult decision—but I wonder if I would be selecting it only to prove to myself how tough I am? Alternative D would do a lot of good—but is this my true reason for choosing it? Alternative E would be something that I could accomplish fairly quickly and, honestly, I always have been rather impatient. Or should I put on the brakes? And what about my old dream of entering a religious order? Isn't that the most "spiritual" path, wouldn't it somehow be more Christian, more radical, and more valuable?

Inclinations are frequently varied, contradictory, and confusing. We acknowledge them, accept them, and evaluate them. Following an old tradition, Ignatius refers to them as "spirits": This image distinguishes a good spirit from an evil spirit. A good spirit or angel whispers feelings and thoughts into the searching person's ear, and shows him or her which way is good and beneficial. An evil spirit, or demon, whispers things that will entangle him or her in disaster, frequently without the person immediately noticing it. One can also speak of voices. They flatter or entice, they dispute or justify, they instill fear or inspire enthusiasm, they slow down or urge forward, cause desire or revulsion, tears or laughter, talk sense or nonsense. We must discern these voices, that is to say, we must try to detect if they lead us to evil through lies and deception, or if they are guiding us toward good with unadulterated truth.

Ignatius calls the ability to discern the spirits "prudence" (in Spanish, *discreción*). Prudence includes a proper balance between closeness and distance to material and spiritual things, sensitivity and tact, clarity of thinking and proper standards, affective maturity and life experience, soberness of mind and the ability to be enthusiastic, discretion and honest communication. Everything that strengthens prudence helps us practice the art of discernment. Those who consider themselves lacking in prudence or those who are told by others that they are acting imprudently would do well to seek the advice of and help from a prudent person.

The Rules for the Discernment of Spirits (SE 313–363) are a complicated section of Ignatius' work. This book is an attempt to take the important aspects of the rules and make them applicable to contemporary situations. Chapters 3, 4, and 6 will adapt some of the rules to our contemporary situation.

CHAPTER THREE

THE CRITERIA FOR DISCERNMENT

Are there any clear criteria that can provide certainty when we are making important decisions about our lives? Unfortunately the answer is both a yes and a no. Yes, there are several criteria that are helpful and can provide guidelines when making a decision in a complex situation. But no, these criteria are not simple devices one can apply to come up with a safe and sure decision.

Decisions are always a matter of the mind and the heart: One must adjust existentially to the concrete, frequently unsatisfactory and unclear situation. One must weigh inclinations and arguments, a process that is always accompanied by an inexplicable, affective component. Criteria must be employed, some of which will always and necessarily be subjective. One must struggle, personally and often in solitude, toward a decision that will never be entirely sure or predictable. One must be prepared to take risks.

The criteria we use in discernment are based both on our values and on our image of humanity in which those values are rooted. They are always socially, culturally, and religiously determined. And much of this is the result of our history. However, in our pluralistic world, the obligatory canon of rules and values has dissipated to the point where many people feel disoriented and no longer able to make decisions. Apparently even our Christian values can no longer be defined with the kind of clarity that will suffice for many. The reflections presented in this book take their directions from biblical and Christian values and presume—not immodestly—that these are the best values for *all* of humanity. In the following, some criteria of discernment shall be developed based on the Christian, particularly the Ignatian, tradition.

THE IGNATIAN "MORE"

Presumably, people who wish to make a decision have somewhat freed themselves, i.e., they have become indifferent in the Ignatian sense. They have examined if their hearts and minds contain inclinations tempting them to seek their own advantage at the expense of other people. Once they have detected such inclinations, they have made an effort to keep them from determining their actions. They have rejected what these disordered inclinations—these "evil spirits"—are "whispering" into their ears. As far as their discernment is concerned, they have eliminated as much as possible those possibilities that could lead to evil.

Several good alternatives still remain for consideration. People will then want to determine which alternative will be better. This sentence contains a comparison. What will bring more? Which alternative is the greater, more fulfilling, and more effective one with respect to good? Ignatian spirituality refers to this criterion of selection using the Latin word for "more," *magis*.

Of course, this more depends on a determination of its content: What is this thing we desire more? How should what was selected lead to more? These questions deal with the goals one strives for throughout one's actions. These goals are preset for Christians: They are peace and justice, the central values of what Jesus called the kingdom of God. According to Paul, one may add: faith, hope, and love (1 Cor 13:13). Thus any activity promoting these values to a greater degree should be selected. As already mentioned, we can also look to Jesus and follow his example: his mercy, his faithfulness, and his courage, his magnanimity and his love. These values are our primary and most important criteria. Whenever we are facing a decision, we should take a look at these values, profoundly meditate on them, and internalize them through our relationship with Christ. It would also be prudent to privately define these goals in personal and more concrete terms. Notes about the following questions may be helpful: What do I desire? What do I want to make of my life? How do I define the goals of my life?

When zeroing in on a concrete decision such as the choice between two career alternatives, one can ask: Which of the two alternatives—

given my talents and my limitations—will provide me with an opportunity to contribute more
to efforts of making the world a bit more just,
peaceful, filled with love, merciful, faithful, and
hopeful? A woman confronted with the question
of whether or not she ought to get married can
ask herself: Considering the story of my life, my
personality, my psychological and physical talents and limitations, which form of life will let me
contribute more to the growth of love and justice
in my immediate surroundings? Of course,
nobody will respond to these questions in simple
terms because, as long as the decision is between
two alternatives that are good and just, every
career will contribute to the kingdom of God.
One can live in love and serve justice in every
walk of life. Objectively speaking, the choices
carry fairly even value. What matters more is
one's subjective contribution: What constitutes
my more? Others will then find their more.

Being able to differentiate between goals and
means is important in the eyes of Ignatius: Goals
are content-based values. We desire them
because they are good in themselves; God wants
them because he has only our and the world's
best interests in mind. The divine order of cre-
ation has preordained them for us. However, we
must always select anew and concretely the
means that help us reach these goals: career
activities, tasks, and projects, but also states of

life such as married, single, or religious. We must not seek them as if they were goals in themselves, since that would attribute independent value to them, thus rendering them absolute. Insofar as they are means, they ought to be valued highly and cultivated and chosen with a view to which are more helpful, more effective, and even better poised to allow one to reach one's goals. We are invited to search for greater engagement, greater challenges, and a possibility for greater dedication.

Many people have misconceptions about the Ignatian more. They are misled by the mentality of needing to be doers, causing them to work more and harder and under greater pressure—perhaps in order to redeem the world single-handedly. Or they force themselves to perform deeds that exceed their strengths, making them sick. Correctly understood, more is a contribution to work that is essentially accomplished by another person. This person may need the hands of brave fellow workers, but the success of the whole project does not depend on these workers. Therefore one must be careful not to demand too much of oneself and to take measures against doing so in a timely fashion. God never makes excessive demands on anybody. That is why human beings should engage themselves according to their individual strengths and abilities. We need to constantly check our actions in order to avoid any tendency to do too much or too little. Doing too much is currently more fashionable. As long as we have done everything we possibly can, we may take a rest and turn our responsibilities over to others, even if it might seem that nobody will be picking up the slack.

THE FIRST MAIN CRITERION: GREATER FRUITFULNESS

In using this criterion we ask: Which alternative produces better results, i.e. more fruit? Which alternative provides me with an opportunity to do good for myself and for my fellow human beings? Which alternative will be more effective, more beneficial to, or more productive for myself and for others? Yet how am I to know which path will bear more fruit ten or thirty years from today? May I trust my hunches? What does "fruit" actually mean?

The criterion of fruitfulness refers to the values enumerated in the previous section. It serves, as it were, as the objective criterion when the one who makes a selection places himself or herself second to others, thinking, "What will bring more for all of us?" One could refer to it as the selfless, altruistic criterion. Being Christian demands that we act with this perspective in mind: Out of love for our neighbor, we are supposed to go the limit for others. We are to give: of our riches, of ourselves.

Fruit does not refer to a measurable result. "Success is not one of the names of God," stated Martin Buber famously. It is easy for us to succumb to the temptation of valuing external, material, and measurable results too highly. It is easy for us to yield to worldly values: money, power, luxuries, prestige, etc. The evil spirit keeps trying—openly or clandestinely—to make us think in these terms and to influence our decisions accordingly. Fruit suggests different values: community-based activity, the reasons behind the obvious, and whatever possesses lasting value; what is written between the lines; hidden beauty and hidden paradise; the small, but personal, steps toward reconciliation or justice. Fruit means depth more than abundance, quality rather than quantity. Fruit does not represent what flatters above all the ego of those who are responsible for producing it, but it primarily honors God. Irenaeus of Lyon, one of the fathers of the church, once said: "The human being fully alive is the glory of God." Fruit is what *human life* makes possible and allows to blossom.

In making important decisions, we can't know with certainty which alternative will produce more fruit during the course of a long life. All that matters is that we decide unemotionally and humbly which of the alternatives might presumably be the better choice. There is no need here to be smarter than we possibly can be. It will suffice to conscientiously examine our alternatives while keeping this question in mind. We depend on the Spirit and trust the action of the Spirit in situations where we are merely capable of weighing the issues. And we hope for the best. And even if in time we discover that the fruit was less than expected, it will ultimately be no longer our responsibility.

THE SECOND MAIN CRITERION: GREATER SPIRITUAL CONSOLATION

The next question we ask ourselves is: Which of the alternatives offers more joy, peace, and fulfillment? Which one lets me be myself more, gives me a greater sense of identity, and makes me feel content with myself? Which alternative pulls me more toward good and life-giving relationships with myself, my fellow human beings, and God? Which alternative allows me to express my feelings more freely, to overcome my sufferings, and savor my joys? But we must also ask: Can I trust my expectations about what will happen ten or thirty years down the road? What does spiritual consolation really mean?

The criterion of spiritual consolation reiterates the values mentioned above, but now they apply more to the person who makes the decision: What will bring *that person* more peace and justice, more love and hope? In a manner of speaking, the criterion of spiritual consolation is the subjective criterion that lets the deciding person look out more for himself or herself and for his or her well-being. It is oriented toward the self, in fact it is egocentric. Being Christian necessitates this perspective because, as the second of the two greatest commandments says, we are to love our neighbors as we love ourselves. We are not only to give but also to receive.

Spiritual consolation does not mean primarily fun, the kind of fun that is idolized by our postmodern culture—in the sense of superficial pleasure or instant gratification. Of course, it would be wrong to summarily condemn fun as unchristian. Spiritual consolation suggests rather the kind of fun we refer to as joy. It is a lasting pleasure rooted in values. According to Ignatius, spiritual consolation means love of God and our fellow human beings. It is a genuine relationship that moves and fulfills. It is faith, hope, and charity and "every interior joy which calls and attracts one toward heavenly things" (SE 316). This is what is meant by spiritual experience, by being filled with the Spirit, by the sense of being close to God. Ignatius also describes spiritual consolation as tears of joy or pain over one's personal suffering or that of others. We may be surprised by the mention of this aspect of pain. Yet those who can shed tears over pain or even guilt are undergoing a process of mourning and purification. As long as one mourns, one merely feels the pain. Yet, in the long run, mourning is beneficial, because it reconciles, relieves, and consoles.

Those facing decisions about their lives will have to ask themselves which alternative will continue to offer more consolation throughout their entire lives and which alternative will provide them with greater authenticity and happiness. Only under the constraints of this perspective will they be able to weigh the pros and cons calmly, and to realistically conjecture and hope. Although there is ultimately no certain answer, one can still seek it fervently and finally come to a decision. Subsequent doubt about whether the decision was indeed the right one is met by the assurance that everything possible was done at the time. Thus one may rest assured that, even in this case, God will make the best of the decision.

SERVING OTHERS OR SERVING OURSELVES?

How are the two main criteria related to one another? If we understand them to be extreme alternatives, they seem to contradict one another: Fruit is a good for the benefit of others, while consolation is intended for those who make a decision. What will happen if the alternatives compete with one another, or if they lead to opposite options? For instance, somebody gets a new job offer that will allow him or her to do a lot of good deeds for others, but which will entail many sacrifices and hard work. Were he or she to keep their old job, they would enjoy a quieter, freer, and more fulfilled life, but would end up doing less good for others. What should the decision be?

There is no point in unnecessarily allowing both criteria to compete with one another. The above example looks at the situation rather superficially. As a rule, a task that is beneficial to the person making the decision will also benefit others. People facing decisions ought to choose in accordance with what makes them feel good and consoles them, hoping that this will also do others some good. Both the consolation and the fruit should complement, promote, and permeate one another. The consolation of the one who makes the decision will bear fruit in others and

console them. In this way it will turn into consolation and fruit for them. Only those who possess
something themselves are able to give something
to others, and only those who give to others will
receive something from them. Egoism and altru-
ism ought to offset one another. Living and loving is always also a mutual exchange, receiving
as well as giving (cf. SE 231). Both succeed only
simultaneously and mutually. Even those—as in
the example above—who initially give much and
get little in return will get much in the long run.
Although it may be in a different form, it will
always be more.

In the past, Christian education over-
emphasized giving: One was to always serve, be
there for others, be humble, and sacrifice oneself.
Many older Christians completely internalized
these teachings. Thinking of oneself was considered unspiritual, immoral, and even unchristian.
Now, however, we find ourselves living in the
midst of a self-oriented culture. Ever tougher
competition forces us to see to our own needs, to
build up our identity, to live our own lives. Today,
people are more inclined to look out for themselves, and to do things their own way.

To be a Christian is to combine the two
extremes: The guideline for behavior is not only
service of the other but also appropriate care for
oneself. Yet at the center of one's thoughts and
actions must be not only one's own well-being,

but also the needs and wants of one's fellow human beings. We should love our neighbor as ourselves (Lk 10:27; Lev 19:18). Neither aspect competes with the other, nor do they mutually devalue one another; indeed, they are of equal value. They are to complement, support, and promote one another.

A DOWNWARDLY MOBILE CAREER: POVERTY AS A CRITERION OF DISCERNMENT?

There is still one more criterion to add to these three: "Just as you did it to one of the least of these who are members of my family, you did it to me" (Mt 25:40). Mindful of the meaning of the Ignatian more and the need for more effective orientation toward service, we should begin our examination of this criterion for discernment by reflecting on the experience of those who are farthest from the riches of the kingdom of God, those at the very bottom of our society. The poor, the sick, the downtrodden, the abandoned, the exploited, and the violated all hunger and thirst for justice, love, peace, and salvation. If we help these people who are at the bottom—whether innocently or because of their own actions—we will create fruit and consolation. We should specifically ask ourselves: How hard am I working to lessen human suffering? Am I using all my strength and talents for this? Of course not every Christian ought to become a social worker or work in an agency in a foreign country. But to the extent that one is free to choose a certain career, commitment, or lifestyle, every Christian ought to be willing to ask whether his or her efforts primarily enhance the well-being of the rich and fortunate, or if he or she is also helping the disadvantaged in some way.

Jesus Christ set the example by becoming poor. God's son humbled himself by being born in a manger in Bethlehem. He humbled himself all the way to his death on the cross on Calvary. He blessed the poor in the Beatitudes because the kingdom of Heaven was waiting for them in a special way. He turned to the needy of his time, to the blind and the lepers, to the small people, the children, the widows, and to those who had fallen among the robbers. In the end, he himself was crucified like a common criminal. Jesus identified with the poor and showed solidarity with them even unto death. That is why, even today, we can recognize him in the least of our brothers and sisters (Mt 25:40).

Ignatius, too, served the poor of his day. He took care of beggars and the sick, and with his companions he went to the hospitals to tend to the incurable. During the famine of the winter of

1538–39, he had the needy lodged in houses belonging to the order and founded a house for the socialization of prostitutes.

This prompts the question: Should our decisions be oriented toward the kind of service that is more difficult and causes us to renounce more of our own needs? Should we seek our cross in the sense that we consider it as a more and thus strive for it? Is perhaps carrying a cross a criterion of our discernment? Clearly, there is only one answer: no. Surely Ignatius speaks frequently of the cross, but not in conjunction with making decisions. The cross must not be chosen. For purposes of selecting criteria for discernment it will be sufficient to apply what was mentioned before: Both the fruit and the consolation should be positive values. Renunciation and suffering must not be chosen because they do not constitute any values in themselves. Here, too, we can look up to Jesus who asked the Father in the Garden of Gethsemane (Lk 22:42) to remove the cup of suffering from him. Not even Jesus sought the cross, but "merely" accepted it.

Thus Jesus shows us the proper attitude toward the cross: We ought to be prepared to bear it, *if the Father wants us to*. When and why does the Father wish it? On Good Friday he wanted Jesus to bear the cross because—according to our interpretation of the events—humanity could be redeemed of evil only in this way.

Apparently, somebody had to bear the pain, that is, had to suffer it, suffer through it to the very end, and ultimately remove and destroy it. Jesus took this service upon himself *on our behalf*; as human beings we can help one another because of his sacrifice. Will the Father demand that we bear a cross too? Yes, if and insofar as it will be necessary for a greater service, for the purpose of a "more." It is our obligation only to be *prepared to accept* it. Time and again, Ignatius speaks of "disposability," i.e., availability, another word for the attitude described as indifference earlier. It is difficult enough to even adopt this attitude.

Some examples: A pregnant woman decides to carry her handicapped child to term and to raise it by herself—a personal burden she willingly accepts for the sake of her child's well- being; this she recognizes as the greater good. A single and healthy physician decides to help rebuild a region devastated by war even though he will not make any money and will even risk contracting dangerous infections. A woman, or even more so a man, decides against a career change because family is more important. A priest decides to replace a fellow priest who had been murdered in a slum in Bogotá, Colombia. Although he is fully aware of the dangers awaiting him there, serving the poor is more important to him. Despite having to force herself, an elderly, still spry woman visits seriously ill and lonesome people in a nursing home every afternoon.

In situations such as these some people deprive themselves of a personal good in favor of a greater, social good. They are not looking to do so, but they accept the sacrifice because it is meaningful and necessary for the work. What motivates them? What is their goal? It is probably—in plain Christian terms—their love for the needy and the poor that leads them into a "downwardly mobile career," into a willingness to do with less, and into dedication to and affirmation of the cross. And yet they do not embrace the cross for the sake of the cross. They embrace it because it makes sense as a means of lessening the deprivation of the needy and the pain of the downtrodden, thus helping them to raise up, to heal, and to rescue them.

Do these people therefore deprive themselves of their "consolation" for the sake of a fruit? Once again, the answer will have to be yes and no. First, for the sake of the needy they must indeed let go of some personal satisfaction or sense of security. Yet generous people will always get something in return: a significant encounter, a joyful experience, a consolation, a new fruit. Still, people no longer view serving others for the specific purpose of getting something in return. This perspective is disappearing more and more. They do so exclusively for the sake of the other, needy human being.

Even if much remains unfulfilled in this life, we still believe and hope that everybody—above all the poor—will enter into the fullness of God in their lives. This ultimate perspective makes any service to the poor and needy meaningful, even if it appears that poverty and desolation cannot be overcome in the temporal world.

CHAPTER FOUR

METHODS OF
DISCERNMENT

Now, I finally have criteria for discernment. I understand them, but only up to a point. I thought them over and internalized them. Yet, all this amounts to is just fanciful thoughts. I am still torn. What will it take to come to a decision about my concrete question? Is there anything that will help me get to the bottom of this vexing situation, to sort out my confused emotions? How will I be able to firm this all up without experiencing countless doubts later? Somehow I still want it all. I am afraid of the impending decision because I do not want to give up anything. And I am fearful of having to admit ten years from now that my decision was wrong.

There is no such thing as absolute certainty with regard to any decision one makes. Still, it is possible to accept the risks and approach a decision courageously and creatively. The following methods contribute to the process of discernment, but just as elsewhere in life, methods do not automatically assure success. They provide assistance, but only if they are delicately and patiently transferred and applied to the personal situation at hand. An experienced counselor and an accomplished companion can help us to select prudent individual steps of discernment.

QUIET TIME AND PRAYER

Prior to any public appearance, the great masters of spirituality went into the desert or to some other solitary place for at least a couple of weeks, some for years. This was true of Ignatius of Loyola, Francis of Assisi, St Paul, and even Jesus. Apparently sound decisions are impossible unless one can reflect with a minimum of interruption. We need to pause to bring about a change of scenery. The moment we enter silence, our inner self comes to life: we become more sensitive and more receptive to subliminal messages revealing the things hidden behind the concerns, impulses, motives, and powers that remain otherwise unnoticed. People who are constantly talking and keeping busy never pause to listen. As soon as we turn off the noise, the hustle and bustle of our everyday lives, as soon as we enter a silent state, we can become people who pay attention and who listen.

Of course, during these quiet periods we may also become conscious of the dark elements of fear, disorderly thoughts and urges, hurtful experiences, feelings of guilt, crazy images, chaotic thoughts, and burdens carried over from our past. These are likely to make any discernment more difficult, but we must accept and examine everything in order to gain clarity. If we sweep anything under the rug, it will return in some other form and negatively influence our behavior without our being conscious of it. If the burdens become very heavy, professional psychological help can teach us how to deal prudently with them.

It is helpful to set aside a time for quiet reflection every day, even if this requires us to be more disciplined and organized. Reflecting on a day's events in the evening is important. Many people even set aside a "day in the desert" every month. Prior to any important decision, several days of quiet, or even a week, may be helpful. Perhaps this time can be taken at a retreat center or a monastery. How can we make quiet times more fruitful? Perhaps a spiritual director or a good book will help. Additionally, the following suggestions taken from the Ignatian tradition and specifically designed for situations requiring discernment are useful.

When confronted with impending decisions, I can reflect on the day's events, especially by paying particular attention to my feelings with respect to the upcoming choice: What gets my attention? What excites me? What paralyzes my thinking? What prevents me from moving forward? What prevents me from taking an honest look at reality? Are my fears justified or are they unfounded? What motivates me? Are there any impulses I don't like? What ties me down, what constrains me? Is there anything that could help me become freer? Do I give in too quickly to my emotions, or too slowly? Do I tend to overly rationalize or justify situations, talking myself into action or into suppressing something? Do I pay too much attention to the opinion of other people? What do I truly desire?

Anyone who wishes to deliberately arrive at a Christian decision ought not only to be aware of his or her questions and to reflect on them, but also ought to include them in his or her prayers, that is, by telling God about them during quiet times. There is no way that we will be able to fool God, nor do we need to pretend anything in God's presence. With complete honesty, we should hold up to God our innermost inclinations, even those that annoy us or those of which we are ashamed. Our conversation with God may be direct, lively, even testy—full of questions or even complaints. Many people find it easy to pray following a negative experience. However, the moment things are going well for them, they forget about God rather quickly. We should make efforts to thank God for the good things in our lives, to laud and praise him. Then our lives will be freer, more content, and more joyful.

Anyone facing decisions ought to discuss with God everything that moves him or her: desires and doubts, hopes and fears, feelings of being torn or pressured, and the anticipation of joy and satisfaction. No prayer will change a thing about the concrete situation or the constraints inherent to it, nor should one count on God's direct intervention. Yet prayer changes those who pray. Those who pray become more open to all sorts of possibilities, and in the process, freer. By looking to God it will be easier to forgo a certain alternative and its attractions, to accept reality with all of its inescapable circumstances. Those who pray will be less overcome by paralyzing moods, they will be grateful for everything that is good about their decision.

Prior to making decisions, one can pray using pertinent passages from the Bible. After extensive reflection on the settings and images, one will recognize elements of one's own life in the personages and in the events of the Bible; one will be stimulated, challenged, and consoled by the messages contained in them. We should hold the life of Jesus, as described by the gospels, particularly close while making decisions. The way Jesus conducted himself, what he taught, how he dealt with human beings, how he demonstrated mercy and love: All these will become guideposts for our own conduct. The relationship to Christ that is deepened through prayer will change us and make us receptive. By contemplating holy scripture, our daily reflection will become more direct, more colorful, more lively.

A retreat can be helpful prior to important decisions. During the time spent in the silence of a monastery or a retreat house, we are letting ourselves be guided by the organizers of the retreat while contemplating and praying intensively, guided mainly by texts from the Bible. A companion will help us practice the mechanics of spiritual exercise during private conversations; he or she will offer individual advice regarding any unanswered questions. The distance from everyday life fosters reflection, the quiet atmosphere furthers more profound observation, and the silence prompts personal prayer. Retreats, held in the spirit of the Ignatian method, can be aimed specifically at decisions that will be reached through faith and during a conversation with God. Of course, even if a retreat is made well, it won't be a surefire method of achieving specific results. Still, depending on the situation of those who participate in the retreat, it can provide steps toward clarity in the decision-making process.

Greater Freedom

How can one possibly strengthen the attitudes of inner freedom and receptiveness that create a stance of indifference? In order to become more free, we ought to take care as much as possible not to let ourselves be affected by fears that will restrain us and stand in our way. The same applies to possessions, habits, rituals and fixations to which we cling, which we are convinced we must absolutely have, but which really rob us of our freedom. Additionally, we will be freer throughout the decision-making process if we consciously invite *several* possibilities that all appear reasonably meaningful, fruitful, and viable avenues—even though the level of consolation and fulfillment we experience may vary ("health rather than sickness, wealth rather than poverty" [SE 23]).

Only the decisions of those who select the better alternative from a number of several innately good alternatives are truly free; those who decide between a good and a bad alternative do not choose freely because the bad alternative does not really represent an option. Those who wish to accept several alternatives as good must perhaps exercise their freedom one more time and rid themselves of images created hastily in black and white or of prejudices, of unrealistic fears or of heightened expectations, of so-called "disorderly inclinations," and of bad external or internal influences.

Let us contemplate for a moment the biblical story of the rich man (Lk 18:18–27): He wants to do *more* than what was at his time considered correct from a religious and civil point of view, namely the observation of the Ten Commandments. Jesus advised him to sell his possessions, but he cannot bring himself to do that, and ends up going away sad. We can make an attempt at figuring out which possessions we would have to give up in order to become freer for the decision process: material things, gifts and skills, memories and experiences, satisfactions and relationships, external success and the pride we take in it. In and of themselves, these "things" are not without merit, nor are they bad; quite to the contrary. However, if they constrain us and if they keep us from doing the "things" that help others, they will restrict our freedom. We can pray for greater freedom.

On the other hand, one can contemplate the story of the widow in the temple (Lk 21:1–4): The rich contribute "only out of their abundance," while the poor widow puts "her entire life" (from the original Greek text) into the alms box when she drops in her sole two coins. I can ask myself if and how "my entire life" will be affected and challenged by the impending decision; whether I'm prepared to take a risk, if I want to go the limit, surrendering myself completely. In the event that I should have doubts, I can submit these to God and ask him for better discernment.

One can contemplate the Annunciation in similar fashion (Lk 1:26–38). Mary's words, "Here am I, the servant of the Lord; let it be with me according to your word," express openness and availability, i.e., receptivity. Although Mary had presumably not comprehended the complete significance of the angel's words, she is nevertheless prepared to let God use her and make her an instrument in his plan for all humanity.

The text of the Beatitudes is equally moving (Mt 5:3–12): The poor and meek, the peacemakers and the merciful, those who hunger and thirst for justice, and particularly those who are persecuted for the sake of their beliefs will all be free and "blessed." They are expecting every fulfillment to come completely from God, allowing him to shower them with gifts and to send them out into the world. Their blessedness does not originate from the fact that they are needy, but from the fact that they are free and open and thus ready to be showered by God with gifts.

People who have to choose between two good alternatives are frequently attracted to both of them. Once an alternative has been selected, the other alternative that has been rejected will have to be mourned. People frequently overlook this need for mourning. In the absence of mourning, there will be a tendency to cling for too long to the repudiated alternative. When this occurs, the one is never completely able to enjoy the chosen alternative. Time and again, one keeps returning to the repudiated alternative because it continues to be desired, as if it were a missed opportunity. One who keeps reproaching oneself for having made the wrong decision after all feels dissatisfied, indeed restless, without any kind of inner peace.

Finally, anyone who makes a decision needs to have the courage to say yes to a *situation*. Yet his or her desire will remain forever unsatisfied because of the wish to possess more, including the other alternatives and ultimately *everything*. This yearning, which is ever so deeply embedded in our hearts, cannot be fulfilled on earth, for it is the yearning for heaven. Anyone who makes a decision says yes to a part, a *fragment* of what he or she desires. We must learn to be satisfied with little. If we freely accept these small possessions in our lives, and if we *live* them to the fullest and with all our hearts, what is merely a fragment will be capable of revealing the whole, thus letting us anticipate heaven in our minds. Yet there will remain a certain degree of emptiness, an ultimate lack of fulfillment. Renunciation is a painful form of dying internally. To accept this and to suffer through it frees us to lead a truly human life.

THE PRACTICE OF IMAGINATION

Holy scripture can help us recall how Jesus called the disciples to join him, for instance in Mk 1:16–20 or Jn 1:35–51. We read about it in the calling of Mary of Magdalene in Jn 20:11–18. Old

Testament narratives can also move and stimulate us, for instance Abraham's exodus in Gen 12:1–5, Moses at the burning bush in Ex 3:1–15, the call of Gideon in Jgs 6:11–24, the vision of Isaiah in Is 6:1–13, or young Jeremiah's call and commission in Jer 1:4–10. Each one of these narratives possesses its own perspective and highlights a different point of view. Some appear to us as archaic, even strange. Yet in all these narratives, human beings are touched by God, called, and told what to do. Anyone facing a decision can view his or her decision in the light of one of these narratives. They can imagine how God touches them, addresses them, and tells them what to do. They can present their alternatives to God, permit all their feelings and thoughts to surface, and ask God to reveal which alternative will bring them greater consolation and bear more fruit. They can ask God for a sign: This may happen in the form of a strong inner leaning toward one of the alternatives or an external sign, a sudden clarification or an intuitive insight, an appropriate remark by a friend, or an insight obtained in a moment of silence, i.e., internal or external voices. Thus, one should be receptive during reflection and prayer in order to be able to hear various signals.

A helpful practice in conjunction with weighing two alternatives of a decision can be imagined in the following way: *At first I will contemplate one of the alternatives, imagining where it will lead, staging before my inner eye, as realistically as I possibly can, the drama of this future life: my activities, my relationships, the places I will go in this life, my leisure time activities. I will imagine where this alternative will take me in a year, in three years, in ten years. I try to imagine what life will be like on an average day during any one of these years. If I cannot quite picture a place yet, I will simply imagine several scenarios. I will basically look at this alternative with optimism, as if I were experiencing real fulfillment and finding it to be beneficial. If negative images, fears, or obstacles surface, I will calmly contemplate even those. I can grasp with open arms everything that comes my way, look at it lovingly, and include it in my prayers. I will ask myself if I'm making my choice lovingly. I will find consolation in the chosen alternative, and pray that it will bring fruit. I will write down on a piece of paper anything that comes to mind, every thought and every sensation, perhaps in two columns, separating the positive aspects from the negative ones in conjunction with this alternative.*

Spend a good amount of time, at least an hour, with this first part of the exercise. We can carry these thoughts with us in our daily lives, as if we were "pregnant" with them, weighing them repeatedly during moments when we are not preoccupied.

As soon as you come to a certain conclusion, engage in the same exercises with the other alternative: *I will also imagine the scene of this possibility and I will once again go over it lovingly and optimistically, and as realistically as possible. I will ask myself: Where will this alternative take me in a year, in three years, in ten years? Once again, I will write down everything that comes to mind, every thought and every sensation, even the unpleasant ones. I will question myself about my motives, looking at the sources of consolation and seeking the fruit this alternative will bear. Again, I will pray with everything that comes to mind.*

Take as much time for the second part of the exercise as for the first one. Do not jump back and forth between the two parts, nor between the things imagined, but instead keep the two parts separate. Too early a comparison of the two alternatives will not be very helpful. Only after having learned to appreciate both possibilities as viable will you be able to distinguish between good and better. If one of the alternatives turns out to be concrete and tangible while the other one remains vague and uncertain, do not attach too much significance to this and, instead, try to imagine the features that are missing. After completing both parts of the exercise, look the notes over and carefully compare both possibilities. Try to look past the irrational aspects, i.e., the aspects that are overly frightful or overly enthusiastic, as well as aspects that are overly self-serving. Even as far as thoughts are concerned, unmask and set aside exaggerations, forced justifications, and one-sided rationalizations. A companion can provide important assistance during the process of discernment. The criteria of discernment will be those outlined in the previous chapter: Which alternative do I expect will provide more consolation and fruit?

Frequently this exercise leads to unexpected insights about the existing possibilities. It reduces fears and biases and helps create a neutral and fair valuation. It makes it possible to rate the offered alternatives more in line with the mentioned criteria. Prayer lets us see reality through the eyes of God and it provides us with a sense of direction. Frequently, the exercise will help us to clarify the decision at hand. It may even be helpful to repeat the exercise.

The following could be a supplementary exercise:
Once again, I look at the first alternative. At the same time I will focus on everything I will lose in a comparison to the other alternative. I will therefore contemplate my losses and picture them realistically and quite dramatically. Perhaps, I will be saddened and overtaken by separation anxiety. I will endure this sadness and this fear. I would like to decry the loss. I will reject cheap forms of consolation and entrust my losses to God. For love of what I have chosen I will accept the emptiness that will be connected to it and the unfulfilled desire. I'm confident that I will be able to endure the loss and endure it well. I know that I will receive something different and greater.

This exercise, too, is performed first in conjunction with the one then with the other alternative. Once again, make notes about the thoughts and emotions. Afterwards there will be time to make comparisons. Those who are able to mourn well will sense that the losses are lighter, that is to say, they will be less disconsolate than they had previously pictured in their imagination, which was so often distorted by fears. Those who have suffered through saying no to the one are in a better position to say yes to the other. The losses do not create any criteria for choice, because only the positive goods, which are acquired by choice or which one hopes to acquire, provide valid criteria. And yet, this exercise will be an aid in making up your mind after a long struggle.

Ignatius proposes two additional exercises to use the imagination. In *Spiritual Exercises* 185 he writes,

> *"I will imagine a person whom I have never seen or known. Desiring all perfection for him or her, I will consider what I would say in order to bring such a one to act and elect for the greater glory of God our Lord and the greater perfection of his or her soul. Then, doing the same for myself, I will keep the rule which I set up for another."*

In Ignatius, the "glory of God" corresponds roughly to what is referred to as "fruit" in this book, while "the perfection of his or her soul" corresponds to what is referred to as "consolation." By practicing not to work on a decision for your own benefit but by imagining it to be advice intended for another, unknown human being, you distance yourself from the decision, thus making it more objective, less dependent on subjective moods, be they positive or negative.

The second Ignatian exercise is:

> *"I will consider, as if I were at the point of death, what procedure and norm I will at that time wish I had used in the manner of making the present election. Then guiding myself by that norm, I*

should make my decision on the whole matter"
(SE 186).

Here, Ignatius refers to that hoped-for hour of death when a peaceful, elderly version of yourself returns a fulfilled life into the hands of God. Thus you ask yourself at this point of death in retrospect how you would have liked to have lived your life, or how you would have decided decades ago what course the rest of your life should have taken at a time when this decision was due. Anyone who is preparing directly for the hour of death must let go of everything he or she possessed in life. Once we let go of everything we will be able to see clearly what is truly important. As unusual as this exercise might seem, it nevertheless helps create more freedom to be perceptive and a greater ability to make decisions. Granted, it presupposes a great amount of faith and hope that we will join God in death and receive what we have desired all along. That is why this exercise challenges our faith: Those who believe will be able to accept more freely the losses resulting from the decision and entrust them to God. Those who are perhaps painfully missing such a faith can endeavor and pray that they will obtain it.

CHAPTER FIVE

DIFFICULTIES DURING THE DISCERNMENT PROCESS

While most people will agree that Ignatius' criteria and methods seem to be fairly insightful and sensible, occasionally there will be situations that are not covered by these instructions. For instance, sometimes there are not two or more good alternatives from which to choose freely. Unforeseen or unavoidable circumstances may personally prevent one from making a decision. Complications are common, perhaps even the norm. Some of these will be discussed in this chapter, even if merely writing about them will make it necessary to simplify everything. Real life situations are always more colorful and more complex, more cumbersome but definitely richer. It is often necessary to look for pragmatic solutions to individual situations. These may well be quite original, even unorthodox, but sometimes they are also modest and, hopefully, even simple.

REVISING EARLIER LIFE DECISIONS

A married woman reports: *I have known my husband for fifteen years; we got married ten years ago. At the time, I was completely in love with him. Now our marriage has reached a dead end. We hardly ever talk to each other anymore and have become emotionally alienated from one another. We have two sweet children; but they seem to be the only thing that keeps us together. My husband is totally wrapped up in his work, while I'm frustrated, sitting at home. I have wanted to leave my prison for a while now, and I'm finally seriously considering a separation. Am I permitted to simply renege on my vows? What will happen to the children? People are splitting up everywhere, but that does not necessarily mean that separation is always the answer. On the other hand, the fact that the church simply does not accept divorce as an answer is of no help to me whatsoever. Are there any criteria for this decision? Is there anything that can heal my internal turmoil? Can I go ahead and simply make a different decision, a better decision about my life?*

Priests and religious who are caught up in a crisis, wanting to leave the priesthood or abandon monastic life, face similar situations; or men or women who conclude after several years of employment that they chose the wrong career. Such situations are rather complex. One needs to view each case individually and carefully look for solutions, solutions that unfortunately will almost always turn out to be painful. Quite often people drag out their problems for years in an attempt to salvage what they had chosen at an earlier stage, what they had laboriously achieved and accomplished, and thus avoid ending up as failures. At some point, the suffering becomes so oppressive that a decision will become inevitable. There is no point in analyzing or assigning guilt. One must calmly understand that both sides are more or less responsible, sharing in the factors contributing to the complexity of the situation. As soon as one can honestly acknowledge this, one can begin to look ahead for a solution.

Ignatius treated such problems rather severely (cf. SE 172): Once one has made a life-changing decision, it must not be undone. One is to stay put, suffer the pain, and make the best of the situation. This unconditional position is no longer tenable in our time and age. There are situations that call for separation or re-orientation as the better, or at least the less harmful, solution. Perhaps, one ought not to announce right away that one is making a new life-changing decision, but more simply and humbly, that in rescinding it, one judges the earlier decision as having been wrong. It will then be easier to accept and to suffer through a separation and pain. What could be the criteria for a discernment about if and when such a revision of an earlier decision is necessary and meaningful?

Using the example above, we might identify the following criteria. If the current relationship no longer promises any consolation or future (i.e., fruit), but only pain; if, in retrospect, the earlier decision has turned out to clearly be a mistake that one admits and that one would not repeat in the future; if the consequences for the people affected by the fallout—the suffering of the children, a breach of confidence vis-à-vis family or friends—are carefully weighed and the damage caused by the separation will not outweigh its benefits; if the spirits were discerned in the sense that one has checked oneself honestly and humbly for signs of subtle narcissism or some other form of self-centeredness; if all these factors add up, then a separation can probably no longer be avoided and will be literally necessary to avert future trouble and suffering. The fundamental rule here is that the earlier relationship—especially if it involves an intimate human bond or a sacrament—takes precedence. Thus there must be salient reasons *for* choosing a separation, reasons so significant that they will outweigh any earlier, higher priority.

After a separation, it will frequently be more prudent to refrain from immediately committing to a new relationship. The soul needs time—sometimes years—to get over a separation, to make the break internally and to refocus. One also ought to separate the two processes—severing the old ties and becoming attached again—in terms of time. Anyone entering into a new relationship too quickly will run risks, for instance, he or she may likely repeat old mistakes unwittingly. Or he or she may take advantage of the new relationship to escape the pain resulting from a separation, so that the new relationship will be chosen for secondary reasons. After a separation—be it in the form of a divorce or of leaving one's vows—people faithful to the church are often facing the problem that, from a canonical perspective, they are in an unsatisfactory state to live an active Christian life within the church. But the real issue is not their canonical status, but how they will work out this tension in the future. Will it be enough to try to contend with the future with only the usual, purely pragmatic solutions?

TRAPS AND PSYCHOLOGICAL ISSUES

People facing decisions should be aware of their individual traps. The following questions may be helpful in identifying those traps:

- Do I tend to commit too quickly? Or, alternatively, do I have a tendency to procrastinate and postpone, to drag out decisions?
- Am I inclined toward childlike or compulsive conformity, or to subservience? Do I tend toward adolescent rebelliousness or a desire to be different?
- Do depressive moods make me see everything in a bleak light, paralyzing me from acting?

- Do I tend toward an exaggerated sense of self-worth and to dreams of being a hero? Or, on the contrary, do I have feelings of inferiority?
- Do I have a tendency to cut myself off from other people? Or do I take refuge in being overly social? Do I gravitate toward dependencies of any kind?
- Do I tend to be hyperactive? Or do I have a tendency to lack motivation or to run from situations and responsibility?
- Do I tend to have an excessive need for being admired?
- Do I have a tendency to suppress reality in order to flee into beautiful, perhaps pious dreams? Or, on the contrary, do I tend to stare pessimistically, perhaps cynically, at the evils of the world so that I can no longer believe in any ideals?
- Do I have a tendency to exaggerate fears, or on the other hand, to being naive or a daredevil?
- Am I given to spiritual fervor or to skeptical behavior that borders on a lack of faith?

The list could go on and on. Every person has their own personal "traps" in which they can get caught. Yet the fact remains that only those who make mistakes will learn something; only those who dare will mature as a result of the *experiment*—an important word in Ignatius. As maturing or mature human beings we learn, often laboriously and never completely, to be aware of our traps. At first, we will be frightened by them and suffer because of them. Yet, after a while, we should pay greater attention to our traps in everyday matters and practice how to skillfully deal with them, that is to say, to deal with them as often as possible. We will also want to make a habit of prudently steering against them—another Ignatian concept. Prudence requires also a certain degree of levity and—a wonderful gift—humor: We can make light of our traps and, as it were, jump over them.

However, if the traps become overly powerful, and if neither humor nor purposeful counter-steering can control them, and if they constantly affect our behavior negatively, an even greater psychological impairment may be at play. In such a case it may be advisable to get professional advice from a psychologist. Those who are troubled by this possibility can go ahead and seek counsel about their very doubts. Those who consistently have a difficult time making decisions, but refuse to admit that they have psychological problems, would do well to seek counseling about the need for or the kind of counseling he or she ought to get. To seek psychological help is not shameful; rather it is honorable for a person to face his or her problems squarely and take remedial measures. The result will not only be a greater degree of self-satisfaction—a greater degree of consolation—but also a greater opportunity to fulfill one's mission in this world. In other words, one will harvest a greater amount of fruit. As a rule, anybody who clearly experiences psychological difficulties prior to important decisions should get therapy *ahead of time*, even if this process may turn out to be laborious and take some time—perhaps even years. After that, he or she will be able to concentrate on the decision more freely and be in a better position to make it.

MAKING DECISIONS IN TIMES OF PERSONAL CRISIS OR UNDER TIME PRESSURE

I'm not feeling well these days. I'm sleeping poorly. I feel like somebody has beaten me over the head, I'm restless and nervous. I often feel sad and depressed, discouraged, and at times desperate. I'm burying myself in work; I hardly ever meet friends anymore and do not feel like talking about my problems. I frequently feel lonesome and empty. There was a time when I was setting some quiet time aside for meditation every day. Now I can no longer find peace during that time, and most of the time I do not even take the time anymore.

Personal crises often show up as physical symptoms: nervousness, sleeplessness, or digestive and intestinal problems. One may be able to suppress dark feelings of grief, rage, emptiness, desperation, or loneliness, but the physical signals will be unmistakable. Such crises also manifest themselves in disordered relationships. They cause tensions, resentment, belligerence, and withdrawal from people. They are often paralleled by a spiritual crisis: Prayers become dry and empty, meditations no longer appear meaningful, and one begins to lose interest in God who appears distant and unapproachable, perhaps even threatening or unjust. Ignatius calls this crisis "spiritual desolation." We frequently describe these symptoms of a crisis as physical and emotional restlessness. Psalms 42 and 43 express these feelings powerfully and prayerfully.

The best advice Ignatius has for someone at this stage of a crisis is not to make a decision at such a time. Those who are not in touch with themselves, with others around them, or with

God can be influenced all too easily by the evil spirit. Those who cannot communicate cannot listen, neither to good counselors nor to God. Despite all the misery crises create, it is helpful to remember that they are often normal and healthy. Through them, we grow and mature, even if we remain unaware of it for as long as we are enmeshed in a crisis. Anyone who is stuck in a crisis ought to focus on making an effort to get out of this state before he or she even considers making a decision. Only those with a well-disposed, joyful disposition full of consolation can acknowledge the reality of things accurately and correctly discern the spirits. In the presence of a good predisposition, one can decide in favor of good, positive things backed by sound motives. Lots of things can help us escape a crisis—a retreat, a vacation, or simply getting some distance from certain people while getting closer to others. Likewise good friends, prayer, and medical, therapeutic, or spiritual aid can make a big difference.

What will happen if one remains stuck in an abortive, unsuccessful long-term situation and if this situation is the cause of the crisis? An example would be the aforementioned marital crisis. The first thing one will need to change is the situation—which will require a decision—in order to get out of the crisis. While this observation may seem obvious, remember that even in a situation like this it is advisable to refrain from immediately reversing a previous life decision. For instance, a woman caught in an unhappy marriage can begin by permitting herself limited time-outs in order to reach inner peace again, away from her husband, and thus draw nearer to a decision. It is important to create as much physical and temporal distance from the situation that created the tension as possible, in order to find oneself and re-establish one's relationship with God.

Still, there are situations that do not seem to leave room for even that possibility. For instance, someone cannot simply forget about a catastrophic situation at work for months because he or she must earn a living or fulfill a contract. In a marital crisis, the wife cannot simply walk away and leave her family in the lurch. One has no choice but to work out a decision while still in crisis in cases such as these. It is true that if one cannot see a way out of a crisis after a lengthy period of suffering, after having examined oneself repeatedly, and after having sought good advice, an abrupt solution may be the only answer. It may be necessary to give notice at work, move out of the house with or without the children, and move in with relatives or into some other place. Such a break will be painful, but sometimes it is the only way to freedom. It won't solve the problem, but it will create the distance necessary to think about a solution. The social consequences will certainly be burdensome, but they may turn out to be the lesser evil.

An additional complication that is often tied to a personal crisis is the pressure of time.

- *Because my girlfriend got pregnant, we had to make a lot of decisions quickly.*
- *After hesitating for years, I can no longer justify postponing my final vows.*
- *This summer I will finish up my studies, and it is about time that I get a grip on finding a job.*
- *My boss wants to know right away if I'm willing to take on the new assignment.*

External, pre-established time frames are frequently at odds with the slower, inner clock. If time pressure is added to the crisis and subsequently heightens it, many people are in danger of collapsing. What to do?

At first, one can try to reduce the pressure of time by refusing to become intimidated by the "just-do-it" craze and hectic pace of our modern world. One can take only small steps in pre-established time intervals, or one can refrain from unnecessary activities in order to create time for quiet reflection. Slowing down can lessen the risk of missing out on opportunities. Once one has achieved some peace, one ought to divide the decision-making process into little steps and devise a time frame for them. A methodical approach can help make the most of a relatively sparse amount of time. Those who do not possess inner peace ought to do everything to find it as soon as possible. Those with a tendency to procrastinate can perhaps interpret time pressures as an opportunity. Used fearlessly and prudently, the pressure can sometimes lead them toward the desired clarity. On the other hand, those who have a tendency to make rash decisions but who typically do not feel pressured, are frustrated by long waits. They can take advantage of a predetermined time frame. It may encourage them to prudently delay a decision and lead to a point where they will approach the decision more level-headedly and with a greater degree of maturity.

WHAT IF ONE'S INTENTIONS REMAIN CHAOTIC?

I have always wanted to become a priest. But to be perfectly honest, I must admit that my motivation is questionable: I'll admit I'm looking for the grand entrance, for admiration. I want a secure job and good income, but I'm running away from the rough-and-tumble workaday world. And, to my dismay, I have recognized that, deep down, I'm afraid of a close partnership. This is something the priesthood would spare me from. Earlier, I cultivated rather spiritual motives: to promulgate the faith, to serve other people, to work for the church. Of course, I continue to harbor these motives to this very day. Yet I'm no longer that enthusiastic about them, I have become more sensible. Now that I have discovered this new layer of questionable motives hidden beneath my former, more noble motives, I wonder if these original motives are still genuine. This is so chaotic! How can I bring order out all of this, how can I bring light into this darkness? Should I seek ordination?

Should I marry my fiancé or not? When we fell in love, I was mad about him and he was the love of my life. Now I see everything much more realistically. I know his foibles and I'm also aware of where and when he will get on my nerves . . . for the rest of my life. Yet, I won't be able to find a better partner any time soon. And as far as the externals go—his career, the house, the money, our families—everything fits perfectly. And I would like to have children as soon as possible. These motives have become very powerful lately. Is love the only thing that is important? Should I go ahead and marry him, or what should I do?

Those who are honest will likely encounter dilemmas like these, because every human being possesses a medley of motives and rationales for the things he or she would like to do. Among them are honest, candid, pure motives and dishonest, impure, selfish motives. Most of them are hardly distinguishable from one another because the motives are like a chaotic bundle, and if we wished to find out which motive belonged to which category we would hardly be able to undo the tangle or to see through it. What do we need to do in order to arrive at certain decisions when faced by unclear or chaotic motives?

We should remember above all that the *positive* motives are important. That is to say, the motives we consider as impeccable and unselfish: love, mercy, dedication to service, the desire for consolation and fruitfulness. Are these strong motives? Are they so strong that they will carry us a good distance? A candidate for the priesthood should ask himself: Will my humanistic and spiritual motives carry me throughout a long life as a priest in spite of all my weaknesses and my feelings of ambivalence? How will I be able to strengthen them? And the bride-to-be can once again look at her love asking herself: Will I be able to say yes definitely, lovingly, and joyfully to this man and my life with him?

The secondary motives—the tendency to flee into a safe situation, the comforts of income and recognition, the middle-class rituals—are then less significant. Whether they each turn out to be morally good or bad can hardly be determined at this point, and ultimately will be unimportant. We need to watch them carefully, but we need not analyze them individually. Nor do we need to suppress them. They will become integrated in due course. God knows how to convert dubious and chaotic energies into something good—when it comes to this, he has a lot of tricks in his bag. We should promote the good in our souls instead of fighting what is unclear or evil. Ignatius says: We should not reach decisions based on disordered affection (cf. SE 21), but we should yield to ordered affections. In the end, God will—as the parable of the weeds among the wheat reminds us (Mt 13:24–30)—tear from our hearts and destroy the evil that we are neither capable of removing nor in need of eradicating.

What will it take to promote the good motives and affections? We can concentrate on real values and practice them throughout our lives; we can seek contact with great human beings and let ourselves be influenced by them; we can stay away from those places and people who promote chaotic and sinful energies; we can strengthen in ourselves the good forces by reading good books, by engaging in personal conversations, and by looking up to exemplary human beings; we can hold ourselves up in prayer to God and ask him for change; we can put our lives in order during quiet times or retreats and let God's grace do its work.

CHAPTER SIX

THE TEN GUIDING PRINCIPLES OF DISCERNMENT

In conclusion, here are ten guiding principles that sum up and expand in greater detail the thoughts that have been discussed thus far. People facing decisions will be able to utilize these guiding principles, checking the areas of their strengths and weaknesses. The strengths should be encouraged while the weaknesses should be carefully observed and, where possible, antidotes should be devised to minimize their impact.

1. STAY IN TOUCH WITH REALITY AND WHAT IS REALLY GOING ON. PAY ATTENTION TO ITS CONCRETE ASPECTS, EVEN TO THE SMALL THINGS.

Every decision requires a settlement of some kind with the preexisting conditions. The reality that already exists must be acknowledged and its value appreciated. This stance is a kind of obedience to reality, and it may be the primary and most important form of obedience. Reality sometimes conflicts with our ideals. Young people often live more in accordance with their ideals than within the confines of reality. While ideals are important and appropriate, we must make certain that they relate to reality in ways that are exciting, innovative, and fruitful. Older people are frequently living in the past, tending to glorify, but sometimes condemning, it. It is likewise important to bring the past into a fruitful relationship with the present. Both require practice. Our images, fantasies, daydreams, thoughts, and feelings must be related continuously to reality in order to make them relevant. The practice of recalling the events of the day in the evening can help us become more aware of reality in terms of greater honesty, sensibility, humility, and love. Such a review will help us to affirm reality honestly and with a greater sense of commitment—just the way it is and not how it was or how we would like it to be. Indeed, those who learn to be attentive and faithful in small things and in everyday affairs will be able to act similarly when larger issues must be faced.

2. DEVELOP AN APPROPRIATE INTERNAL SENSE OF TIMING: DO NOT ACT IN TOO MUCH HASTE, BUT DO NOT DRAG OUT DECISIONS EITHER. ACCEPT EXTERNAL TIME PRESSURE AS WELL AS HUGE DELAYS WITH PRUDENCE. BREAK DOWN YOUR DECISION-MAKING PROCESS INTO STEPS AND PUT THEM ON A REALISTIC TIMETABLE.

The soul has and needs rhythms of its own. Knowing how to manage our time is an important part of the art of living prudently and well. If our souls are kept from adhering to their rhythm, we will make mistakes, even during the discernment process. If we lose our way—whether by adhering to the wrong kind of clock or in some other way—we should recognize that and steer back on course, gently yet with great determination. Throughout the decision process, we must pay attention to timing. Thus before, during, and after a decision, one should feel fundamentally at peace with oneself, that is, consoled. Sudden insights can be good, yet they should be confirmed in everyday life over a longer period of time, judging how much consolation and peace they yield. Flashes of enthusiasm are not good signs if they end quickly in a sense of frustration and emptiness. To be sure, the individual steps of discernment must be ordered and subjected to a time plan, but it should not be overly rigid or ambitious.

3. PLACE YOUR THOUGHTS AND PLANS BEFORE THE CRITICAL EYES OF YOUR FRIENDS. SEEK THE ADVICE OF PRUDENT PEOPLE. EXAMINE YOUR ALTERNATIVES BY TESTING THEM AGAINST EXPERIENCE.

According to Ignatius, the "evil spirit" resorts frequently to the particularly clever tactic of talking people into maintaining secrecy about the plans they are making. To be sure, the pangs of a bad conscience can lurk beneath the desire to conceal one's plans. On the other hand, people who talk about their plans with friends and counselors invite their common sense, their prudence, and their experience into the conversation. Those who are well acquainted with us, especially if they possess a keen sense of judgment, will often be in a better position to recognize our strengths and weaknesses than we will ourselves. Thus they see through our traps and recognize a false conclusion more quickly. If we can't find a friend or counselor, we should formulate our thoughts and plans for a fictitious listener or for ourselves. Sometimes doing this can actually help clarify matters. Prior to any important decision we should also test the alternatives in a practical way, putting them through a test run. This test run can help us come to a decision. Nevertheless, practical experience doesn't always yield certainty. Even

Stefan Kiechle, S.J., Ph.D. in Theology, was born in 1960. For most of his life he has been involved in campus ministry and has been serving as Master of Novices. He resides in Nuremberg

Following three years of studying theology at the Universities of Freiburg and Jerusalem, he entered the Jesuit novitiate in 1982. He continued his studies in philosophy and theology at the universities of Munich and Frankfurt on Main. He received his Ph.D. in Paris with a dissertation about Ignatius of Loyola. After completing his tertiary education in Chile, he served as director of campus minister at the University of Munich. Since 1988, he has been Master of Novices for the German Jesuits in Nuremberg, Germany.

Another Title in the
Ignatian Impulse Series

*These brief, readable, engaging
books present the spirituality of
St. Ignatius as a practical resource
for spiritual seekers of all faiths.*

The Sevenfold Yes
*Affirming the Goodness of Our
Deepest Desires
Ignatian Impulse Series*
Willi Lambert, S.J.
At the heart of spirituality is a yes to
life. **The Sevenfold Yes**, an affirmation
of life's goodness and meaning, is at
the very center of the spirituality of St.
Ignatius whose motto was to "find God
in all things." Lambert invites readers
to reflect on what they consider to be the very best aspects of
their lives and to say yes in a new and deeper way to them.

Each chapter corresponds to a particular part of the Spiritual
Exercises, making this an excellent introduction for the new-
comer or a companion book for the retreatant. Practical prayer
exercises and insightful reflection questions help the reader to
recognize God's call in the desires of one's heart and in the
events of everyday life. Retreat directors, too, will find this a
helpful resource.
ISBN: 1-59471-034-1 / 128 pages / $9.95

KEYCODE: FØAØ1Ø5ØØØØ

with the best counseling and after a number of tests against real life, some uncertainty will often remain. That's why, sooner or later, we simply have to jump in, no matter how cold the water!

4. LISTEN TO WHAT YOUR MIND, YOUR HEART, AND YOUR INTUITIONS TELL YOU. MAKE SURE ALL THREE OF THESE VOICES FROM YOUR SOUL ARE PART OF THE FINAL DISCERNMENT.

Materialism, functionality, and rationality are the basis of our modern world. While we may simply want to condemn these values, we must recognize that, whether we like it or not, much of our everyday lives has to function in accordance with these realties. Yet during important decisions, we must not allow these dominating forces to outweigh other values. We must pay attention to our emotions, appreciate them, and take them seriously—even and especially those emotions that are unpleasant or undesirable. While giving emotions their proper emphasis, we must also recognize that there can occasionally be, especially in religious settings, an overemphasis on emotions. To balance this tendency, we must emphasize that every decision should be made with one eye on material things, functionality, and rational arguments and the other eye on the emotions. In this area, each of us ought to acknowledge his or her tendency to favor one perspective over the other and attempt to take into account and integrate the other side. It may still be possible to reach a decision through a sudden spiritual intuition, but we must be careful to neither undervalue nor overestimate this gift. No matter how a decision is reached, whether in an intuitive moment or over an extended process, we should pray that the decision is confirmed and complemented by the reality it is based in. When this occurs, it is a great blessing. Ignatius' three methods of making choices do not compete with each other, rather, they complement and fertilize one another.

---

5. BE AWARE THAT THE "EVIL SPIRIT" OFTEN INTENDS TO MAKE THE DECISION MORE COMPLICATED THAN IT ACTUALLY IS. HE USES FEAR. SEEK TRUST AND SIMPLICITY.

When trying to make complex decisions, many people get lost in the myriad minute details that require urgent attention. This only confuses them and leaves their head spinning. They are completely unnerved and want to give up. During the decision-making process, we would do well to ask ourselves what the *core* of the matter really is. In the long run, which values and goals—and they may be few in number—are actually involved in the decision? Try to clearly formulate the specific questions one wishes to have answered in the discernment process. Is there a simple tool that will cut a path through the jungle? Try to arrange the many enervating small details around the core and weigh them properly. Occasionally the confusion may reside inside the head, while the heart has already reached its decision. Or the heart may be still wavering, while the mind sees clearly. In such instances, try to steer clear of one's negative tendencies and bring order to the confused part, simply but firmly. A similar tactic works with fears as well. If they are irrational and confuse issues, they emanate from the "evil spirit." We are allowed, indeed we are compelled, to oppose them vigorously and replace them with acts of trust and courage.

6. DO NOT MAKE A DECISION WHEN YOU ARE IMMERSED IN A CRISIS. IN EVERYTHING, LOOK FOR THE GREATER DEGREE OF CONSOLATION AND THE GREATER AMOUNT OF FRUITFULNESS. FOLLOW YOUR DESIRES. BE RADICAL.

When we are caught up in a crisis, we cannot experience consolation. This is not a good time to make an important decision. We will fare better if we wait until the crisis passes to make the decision. Only a person in a peaceful state of mind can judge freely and honestly which alternative will turn out to be the better one. There are two important internal criteria in decision making. The first is the amount of consolation the decision will yield. That is, which alternative will offer a greater degree of inner peace, joy, hope, security, and meaning? The second criterion is the amount of fruit the decision will yield. Which alternative contributes more substantially to justice, peace, faith, and love? Both consolation and fruit complement and permeate one another; they are both comprehensive and fulfilling. At the same time, one must also pay attention to the path which desire points to. When we recognize our heart's desire, we should first cleanse it of any selfish motives and then follow it. Then we may trust that it will lead us in the right direction. Decisions always deal with growth, with the "more." A certain amount of radicality, that is, following the problem to its *radix* (root) and embracing it fervently, comes mostly from the good spirit. However, it must be properly proportioned and without exaggeration.

7. KNOW YOUR LIMITS; ACCEPT AND OBSERVE THEM. DO NOT SEEK THE CROSS, BUT BE PREPARED TO ACCEPT IT OUT OF LOVE IF GOD WANTS YOU TO. GOD'S WILL DOES NOT COME TO US IN THE GUISE OF SOMETHING ALIEN, BUT REVEALS ITSELF THROUGH THE DESIRES OF YOUR HEART, IN THE CONSOLATION AND IN THE FRUIT.

Knowing one's limits and weaknesses and dealing with them prudently is more difficult than commonly assumed. And yet this process is at the core of the human and spiritual maturation process. Self-knowledge requires humility, common sense, and love; it is something we must work on throughout our lives. When we make decisions, we should pay attention to the limits set forth for us, proceeding neither too timidly nor too brashly, using common sense. We must not seek the difficult things in life, the renunciations and sufferings, but we should prepare ourselves to accept them from God's hands when they come to us. The fact that God makes these demands is often difficult to understand and accept. We should accept a cross as God's will only if there are good reasons. The cross occurs more frequently than we would like, because there is evil in the world, and we must accept and suffer through this evil. Whatever God demands of us is shown to us from within. If we recognize another and clearly better way would be to initially accept what we believe is right. Later after the clarification of our motives, we may still want the current path because it is in harmony with our greater goals. Then, we can assume that it is the will of God.

---

8. MOURN THE POSSIBILITIES YOU IGNORED AS WELL AS THE OPPORTUNITIES YOU MISSED. YOUR LIFE IS A PATH OF LETTING GO AND DYING. IF YOU ACCEPT LIFE TO BE THIS WAY, YOU WILL BE ABLE TO COMMIT TO RELATIONSHIPS MORE EASILY AND BECOME MORE CONTENT.

Young idealists want everything, adults attach themselves to some things. If we say yes to one thing, we must say no to another. This no must be accepted fully and consciously. Anything we do not select, we must let go of in our hearts. We will need to mourn it and weep over it in order to be able to accept what we do choose more freely and more gratefully. The older we get, the more things we must let go of, and we must do so more and more without asking any further questions. Every time we let go of something, we die a little. We anticipate our ultimate death as a time when we must let go of everything in order to get back everything and even more. Those who now live with little and live this little to the fullest—"understanding the realities profoundly and . . . savoring them interiorly" (SE 2)—conduct their lives in complete awareness of ultimate fulfillment. They will live with joy and consolation.

9. JESUS SHOULD BE THE NORM, THE PRIMORDIAL IMAGE AND THE "SHAPE AND FORM" OF OUR LIVES AND DECISIONS.

Through Jesus, God has shown us what it truly means to be a human being. The moment we look to him, we can see the guidelines that will lead us on a secure path. Jesus helps us through his teachings—whatever he told and preached to people—through his exemplary conduct and how he dealt with people: mercifully, truthfully, faithfully, fairly, justly, and lovingly. But most crucially Jesus inspires us by the model of the kind of person that he was, by the effect he had and still has on people. The impression his entire being has made on our lives and the manner in which we are being changed in accordance with his image result from our repeatedly looking to him and knowing and loving him ever more profoundly (Cf. SE 104). Frequent reading and contemplation of the gospels in our daily lives and during extended quiet times help us shape our lives in accordance with Christ's image.

---

10. ONCE WE ARE INVOLVED IN THE PROCESS OF MAKING A DECISION, WE WILL REACH A POINT WHERE "THE GORDIAN KNOT" MUST BE CUT. WE MUST ACCEPT THE RISKS AND LET GO. ONE'S FUNDAMENTAL TRUST IN LIFE, IN FELLOW HUMANITY, AND IN GOD WILL HELP THROUGHOUT THE PROCESS.

Ever since the days of antiquity, people have told the story of the Gordian knot. The knot had been tied in such a complicated way that no one had ever been able to undo it. The person who could would reign over all of Asia. When Alexander the Great approached the impossible knot, he simply took his sword and cut it in two. Anyone who agonizes too long over a decision because he or she has gotten lost in its complexity and in its details will eventually reach the point when only a clear and determined cut will do the trick. The liberating cut will only be successful if he or she properly discerns the spirits prior to administering the blow, accepts the risks, and waits for the proper moment. And he or she must trust. Even after the cut there will be obstacles that could not have been anticipated, fears to be conquered. The foundation of trust is laid during childhood. If one's childhood lacks a sufficient foundation, it will be necessary to build it laboriously in later life. We must cultivate and strengthen trust throughout our lives. Only those who trust can make decisions. Those who have insufficient trust should remember that trust can always grow. We should pray for trust and for good decisions.